For my grandparents Eric and Norma, with love

First published in 2019 by Child's Play (International) Ltd
Ashworth Road, Bridgemead, Swindon SN5 7YD, UK

First published in 2019 by Child's Play Inc
250 Minot Avenue, Auburn, Maine 04210

Distributed in Australia by Child's Play Australia Pty Ltd
Unit 10/20 Narabang Way, Belrose, Sydney, NSW 2085

ISBN 978-1-78628-187-6
L310818CPL01191876

Printed in Heshan, China

1 3 5 7 9 10 8 6 4 2

A catalogue record of this book
is available from the British Library

www.childs-play.com

Child of
ST KILDA

Beth Waters

Islands on the Edge of the World

This is the story of a little boy called Norman John Gillies. He was born in 1925 on Hirta. Hirta is the largest island of St Kilda, a tiny group of Scottish islands so remote that people call them the 'islands on the edge of the world'. Norman John lived with his parents in a little stone cottage, with views of an endless sea and a huge sky.

He loved playing outside with the other children in the only street on St Kilda! There were no cars going up and down, no shops, no electricity; just a village with 16 cottages, a tiny post office, a church and a school.

One of Norman John's earliest memories was of his mother standing on the wall outside their house, calling to him in Gaelic that it was time to come home for dinner.

Norman John's parents had lived on St Kilda all their lives, and their parents before them. There had been people living on the islands for at least 4,000 years.

Norman John didn't know it at the time, but he was to be one of the last.

Surrounded by the stormy Atlantic Ocean, St Kilda is a collection of tiny, steep-sided islands and sea stacks. The largest island is called Hirta, which is where all the islanders lived.

St Kilda is one of the most remote parts of the British Isles, more than 160km away from the west coast of Scotland. When Norman John was a child, people used sailing boats or steam ships to get there, and the journey could take days. The islanders used to be almost completely cut off from the mainland for at least half of each year, because the crossing was so dangerous in bad weather.

Even today, the journey takes several hours by motor boat, and visitors cannot land if the wind is blowing in the wrong direction.

ST KILDA

ST KILDA

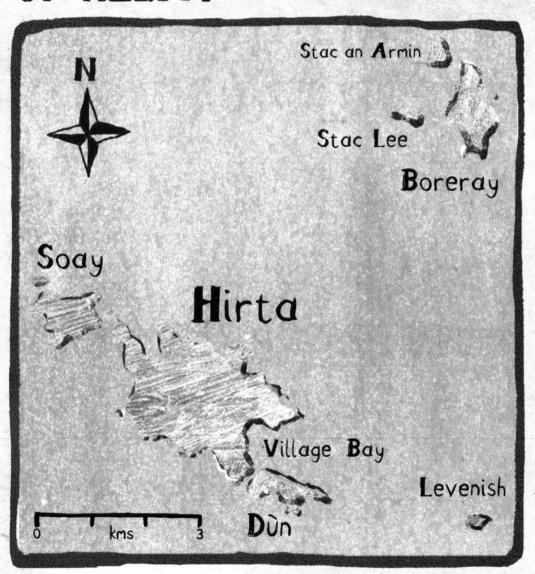

N

Stac an Armin

Stac Lee

Boreray

Soay

Hirta

Village Bay

Levenish

Dùn

0   kms   3

ORKNEY
ISLANDS

RN ISLANDS

SCOTLAND

It is a beautiful, wild and mysterious place.

Sea Birds

St Kilda is home to nearly a million sea birds, which nest on the huge cliffs and hunt for fish in the stormy waters.

Puffins live most of the year out at sea, but they visit St Kilda from April to July each year. They nest in burrows on the grassy slopes of Dùn. Their stubby wings allow them to swim underwater, and in the spring nesting season their beaks develop their famous bright orange and red colours.

Northern fulmars are related to albatrosses and also spend most of their lives at sea. They breed on St Kilda between March and July, building their nests on narrow ledges on the cliffs. They spit a foul-smelling oil at anything that comes too close.

European storm petrels also nest on St Kilda. Despite their small size, they will fly in the roughest weather, often pattering the waves with their feet. They return to their burrows only at night to avoid predators.

By far the most plentiful bird on St Kilda is the gannet.
These birds mate for life, and there are more than 60,000 breeding
pairs on the islands – one of the largest colonies in the world!
They are huge and noisy, with wingspans of up to two metres.
Gannets catch fish by diving from huge heights, hitting the water
at more than 96 kilometres an hour.

Wildlife

Because St Kilda is so isolated, there are three different land animals living there that are found nowhere else in the world. One of the oldest breeds of sheep, the wild Soay have lived on St Kilda almost unchanged since Neolithic times.

The St Kilda field mice are thought to have first arrived on the boats of early settlers. Because they have no predators on the islands, they have grown to be much bigger than mice in other parts of Britain.

Perhaps the most surprising creatures found only on these islands are the St Kilda wrens. Like the field mice, they have also evolved to be bigger than their mainland counterparts in order to survive the harsh conditions. On calm days, you can hear them singing.

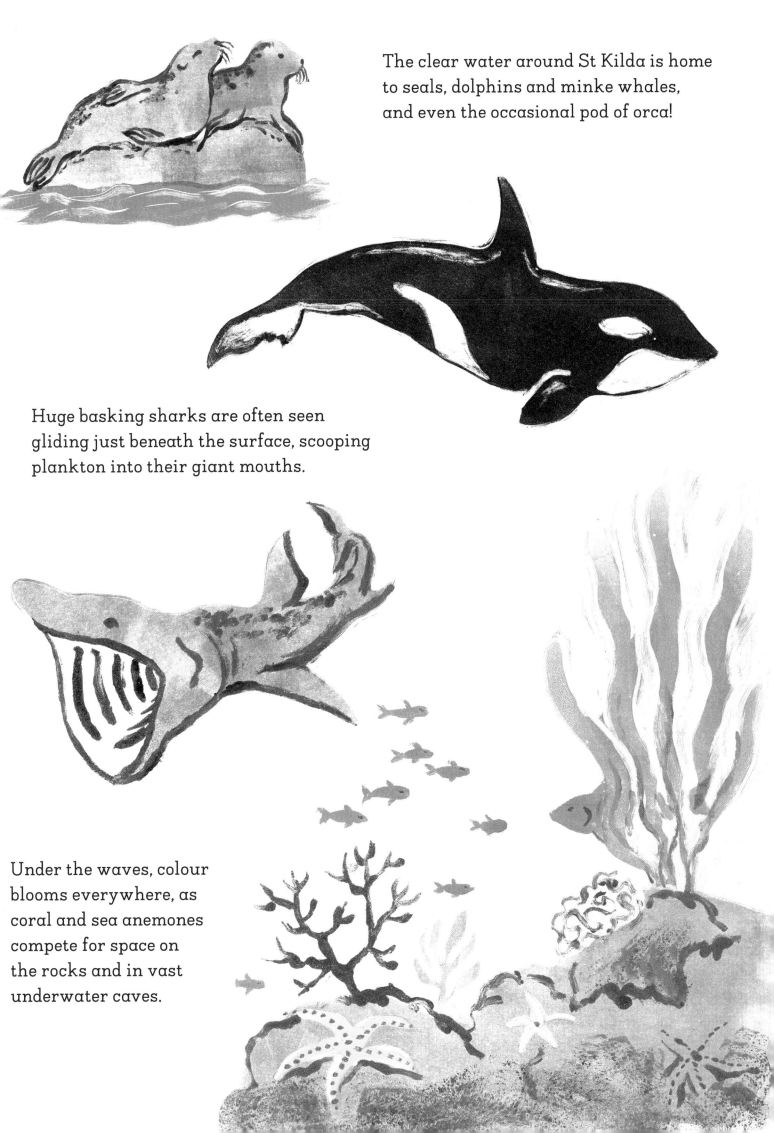

The clear water around St Kilda is home to seals, dolphins and minke whales, and even the occasional pod of orca!

Huge basking sharks are often seen gliding just beneath the surface, scooping plankton into their giant mouths.

Under the waves, colour blooms everywhere, as coral and sea anemones compete for space on the rocks and in vast underwater caves.

Settlers on St Kilda

Until 1930, the 'islands on the edge of the world' were also home to humans. No one knows when the first settlers discovered St Kilda, but they may have either visited or lived on the islands since the Bronze Age, at least 4,000 years ago.

There were never many more than 180 people living on Hirta at any one time, and this had dropped to just 36 by the year 1930.

The first people on St Kilda lived in simple stone dwellings, later building traditional Hebridean 'blackhouses', which they shared with their animals. By the late 1800s, there were 16 small stone cottages on Hirta, built along a single street in the sheltered Village Bay.

Norman John Gillies was born at Number 15 Main Street on 22nd May 1925. When he was first born, he wasn't breathing. The village women tried everything to revive him, including plunging him alternately into hot and cold water, but nothing worked.

His grandmother thought it was time to give up. 'Lay him down,' she said gently in Gaelic, 'for there's no breath.' Then, as a last resort, one of the women gave him a smack on the back – and Norman John began to cry!

His parents named him in memory of two of his uncles, Norman and John MacQueen, who had been tragically lost at sea when their boat capsized. Norman John was always known by both names together, never just by one.

The Families of St Kilda

All the islanders knew each other, just like one big family.
Norman John lived with his parents, Mary and John, in house Number 10.

His Uncle Donald and Aunt Christina lived at Number 13. They had two daughters, Cathy and Rachel.

The MacKinnons at Number 1 were the largest family with eight children!

And at Number 15, where Norman John was born, lived his grandmother, Annie Gillies. She acted as midwife on the island and was affectionately known as the 'Queen of St Kilda'.

Isolation

Until the mid 1900s, the only way to reach St Kilda was by sea. Large ships could not land at all, but had to use small rowing boats to reach the pier. The arrival of a vessel was very exciting and the children would all run down to watch.

St Kilda is exposed to the worst of the wild Atlantic weather.
No trees can grow there because of the wind, which is sometimes
strong enough to blow people off their feet. A severe storm
could leave the islanders deaf for weeks afterwards.

Despite the hardships of living in such an isolated place, the St Kildans lived quite happily, without much interference from the outside world.

Everyone, including the children, had to work as a group to survive in such harsh conditions. The St Kildans were hardworking, generous and kind, and had a very strong sense of togetherness.

There was no need for money and hardly any crime.

Rent to the owner of the islands was paid in feathers, oil and tweed.
Everyone helped each other and made sure that their neighbours
had everything they needed.

What People Did

There were plenty of jobs to be done. Peat had to be dug out of the ground.
Once dry, it was burned to heat the houses.

Every morning, the men would meet between house numbers 5 and 6
to discuss what needed doing that day and who would do it.
This became known as the 'St Kilda Parliament'.

The St Kildans kept a few cows for milk, and blackface sheep for milk and wool. Vegetables, mostly potatoes, were grown for food, as well as barley.

Carding the wool and getting it ready for weaving was a job that took all night, and was accompanied by much singing and merriment.

The wool was spun, dyed and woven into tweed for clothes.

The gannets, fulmars and puffins that live on the islands were very important to the St Kildans, providing food, feathers and oil.

Between the months of March and November, collecting birds and eggs
was the main activity.

The men climbed down the steep cliffs, using nothing but a simple handmade
rope tied round their waist. They caught the birds with a snare and also collected
their eggs. Climbing barefoot gave a better grip, but it was still very dangerous work.
It is said that the ankles of St Kildan men were much thicker than those
of people from the mainland and their toes were much further apart.

The boys started climbing at about 10 years old, which must have been very scary!
Norman John's uncle, Finlay MacQueen, was the best climber of his day.

The whole community gathered to divide the catch fairly among the families, according to need. Everyone was given a share. Each islander was given around 120 fulmars each year to eat — more than two a week!

In 1697, it was estimated that the islanders collected 7,000 gannets in one year, although the number had dropped to around 300 by the 1900s, when 10,000 puffins were also snared every year!

The birds were dried and salted, and kept in one of the specially built storehouses known as 'cleits'. These are completely unique to St Kilda, with more than a thousand of them just on Hirta! The walls were built of stone and the roof covered with turf. The stones had gaps between them so that the wind kept the contents dry, while the turf roofs kept the rain out.

School

All children between the ages of five and fifteen went to school.

They were taught together in one room, which was very cold in winter. The children took turns to fetch peat for the fire. They all looked forward to being called to the front of the class to answer questions, because then they could stand right in front of the warm fireplace!

On the wall there was a map of Great Britain. It left out most of Scotland and all of St Kilda!

When there was a lot of manual work to do on the island, the children were allowed to leave school early to help.

Norman John was never old enough to go to school on St Kilda. Instead, he spent his time playing with his friends. They didn't have many toys, but they had plenty of space and freedom to run around and play games like hide-and-seek.

Norman John was very happy as a child and remembered how kind the islanders were to each other. Once, when he was accidentally burned by some hot peat ashes, almost everyone on the island visited him to make sure he was all right!

Church

Church ministers would come from the mainland to live
and work on Hirta for a while. They were mostly very strict.

On Sundays, no one was allowed to play or even work, because everyone
had to go to church. The services were always long, and Norman John
found it very hard to sit still. His mother had to fetch him from the aisle
every time he tried to get away!

St Kilda Mail

There was a post office in the village, but letters could not leave the island unless a ship came to collect them. Many months could go by without a vessel arriving.

In 1877, some sailors were shipwrecked on St Kilda. Feeding the extra mouths meant that the islanders were soon running out of food.

A visiting journalist called John Sands wrote a letter asking for help and sealed it in a tin, which he put inside a little carved wooden boat. An inflated sheep's bladder was attached to keep it afloat.

The little boat arrived on Orkney nine days later, from where a rescue ship was sent, loaded with food and supplies. After this, the islanders regularly sent out these little wooden boats, which became known as 'St Kilda mailboats'. Some of them sailed as far as Norway!

Visitors

From the 1900s onward, things began to change. New steamships could reach Hirta from the British mainland in a day, so tourists could visit much more easily.

They loved the idea of wild, romantic St Kilda, and treated the locals as curiosities, paying the islanders to pose for photographs. They bought knitted socks, gloves, tweed, eggs and postcards as souvenirs, and the islanders bought sweets and biscuits with the money they received.

The islanders welcomed these outsiders at first, but soon realised that their visitors brought problems. Because the St Kildans were not used to germs from outside Hirta, even a common cold could be dangerous. They would often suffer from a 'boat cough' for days after a ship had visited.

By the time Norman John was born in 1925, the population had already shrunk dramatically.

Visitors told the St Kildans that life was easier elsewhere, so many of the young, able-bodied people began to leave, making life even harder for those left behind.

There was a series of harsh winters when the crops failed and the houses were damaged. The St Kildans were often hungry and cold. They needed food and building materials, but the weather was too bad for boats to bring them.

The isolated islanders also had little resistance to illnesses and many died from diseases brought by the new visitors, such as flu and smallpox.

Too few children were born to build the population and many babies died of a disease called tetanus. New families were brought in from nearby islands like Harris and Skye, but it was not enough.

Waving Goodbye

Then, in January 1930, when Norman John was nearly five years old, disaster struck.

His mother Mary became ill and needed to go to hospital on the mainland. The weather was bad and it was several weeks before a boat finally came to rescue her. Norman John stood on the pier with his grandmother, waving goodbye as the boat carried both his parents away. But help had come too late: Mary's condition worsened and she died in hospital on May 26th.

Years later, Norman John discovered that his mother had been expecting a baby. She gave birth to a little girl, Annie, in the hospital in Glasgow. Sadly, both mother and child died on the same day.

The Evacuation

Norman John's father returned alone, and the St Kildans were devastated. There were now only 36 people left on the islands. Most were either too old or too young to do all the hard work, and help was a long way away.

A visiting nurse called Williamina Barclay was horrified at the living conditions on the island and got everyone together to discuss what they should do.

Reluctantly, all the islanders agreed that the time had come to leave St Kilda. With the help of Nurse Barclay, they signed a petition to the Scottish Office, asking to be moved to the British mainland.

For a while, Hirta was a hub of activity while everyone's belongings were loaded onto a steamship called The Dunara Castle. All the domestic sheep and cows were rounded up and taken away by boat!

Finally, on the 29th of August 1930, a clear
and sunny day, a steamship called HMS Harebell
came to take the St Kildans away to the mainland.

All the houses were left unlocked, with a handful of oats and a bible laid out in each. One of the bibles was left open at the book of Exodus, a story about people having to leave their homeland many centuries ago.

Norman John played on deck with the other children. His saddest memory was of the older people standing at the back of the boat, waving goodbye as their lifelong homes disappeared over the horizon.

With the people gone, the village on Hirta lay abandoned.

As the years passed, the weather destroyed the roofs
and windows of the empty houses, and fulmars
built their nests in the old chimney stacks.

There were no more children to play on the street
or go to the school, and the Soay sheep ran wild.

St Kilda's unique way of life had come to an end.

Afterwards

A few of the St Kildans went their separate ways, but the remaining
28 were all taken to their new home on the Morvern peninsula.
When they arrived, there was a crowd of people waiting on the pier
for a glimpse of these strange incomers. Everything was new
to the islanders, including streets and even motor cars!

The men were given jobs with the Forestry Commission, which they
found very funny as they had never seen a tree before in their lives!
One of their first tasks was to plant new trees on a steep-sided ridge.
None of the local workers wanted to do it because it was so dangerous,
but the St Kildans laughed, saying it was a 'little hill' compared with
the cliffs they were used to. The forest they planted still stands today.

At first the new arrivals were housed separately, but they found
this too lonely, having spent their whole lives together so far. Eventually,
over half were moved into adjoining cottages in Larachbeg. Once again,
Norman John, his father and grandma lived next to Uncle Donald
and Aunt Christina, just like on St Kilda.

Even so, some of the older people never really adapted to their new life.
Granny, who looked after Norman John after his mother died, could never
get used to money. When the barber came to cut Norman John's hair,
she would pay him in hand-knitted socks and gloves!

Today the islands of St Kilda have become a dual World Heritage Site, recognised both for their unique wildlife and vanished culture.

National Trust for Scotland rangers and volunteers live for part of the year in two of the old houses on Hirta. They take care of the islands, looking after the buildings and recording the wildlife.

The British Ministry of Defence has built a radar base on Hirta. It provides the things that the St Kildans never had, like electricity and running water. Boats still bring visitors to see the high cliffs, the sea birds, and the old village where the St Kildans lived and worked for so many years.

Norman John

Norman John himself went on to lead a very happy life. He travelled the world with the British Navy before settling in Suffolk, England, where he married Ivy Knights. They lived in a little house that they named 'St Kilda' and had three children, eleven grandchildren and eleven great grandchildren!

Norman John loved to talk about St Kilda and to tell stories about what life was like there. He went back to Hirta several times with his family to show them the cottage he lived in, the main street and the church where he couldn't sit still. He even helped restore House Number 3, which is now a tiny museum. He wanted everyone to know about St Kilda and what a special place it is!

When he was a very old man, he was able to visit his beloved island home one last time with his son John. He also went to Glasgow, and finally found where his mother Mary and sister Annie were buried. He took some flowers and laid them at the grave. After all those years, he had never forgotten them.

And he loved St Kilda, the wild and beautiful home he left behind when he was just a little boy, for the rest of his life.

Norman John Gillies
One of the last children of St Kilda
22nd May 1925 – 29th September 2013

St Kilda Sketchbook

Friday 2nd June 2017 to Monday 5th June 2017

The hill rises really steeply behind the village.

Gannets – huge noisy and smelly birds! As the boat approached Boreray we could smell the colony, and the rock is white from their poo!

House of the Fairies – one of the oldest structures on St Kilda, a tunnel from the Iron Age! No one knows exactly what it was used for, it was probably a store house.

A St Kilda field mouse got into our food stores! We had to keep everything in sealed containers.

They're big, like gerbils, and not scared of people like normal mice

Sketching on the clifftops in the wind, trying not to drop anything over the edge!

Evening light over Dùn and waves crashing.

Puffin – the Scottish word for puffin is 'tammie norrie' and a baby puffin is called a 'puffling'!

Short wings to allow them to swim underwater. Bright beaks turn dull colour over winter.

St kilda Wren — we saw one singing on a chimney stack. We could hear it better than see it, it was so tiny.

St kilda Church — partly damaged in 1918. A German U-Boat came into the bay and fired shells at the feather store where there was a radio station. Luckily no one was hu

Soay Sheep — no longer found on Soay! After the evacuation they were moved to Hirta and they're still there, completely wild. They're small and look a bit like goats with ragged brown wool. These sheep are everywhere in the old village!

This marks the house where Norman John Gillies lived! After his mother died, Norman John and his father went to live with his granny. No one ever lived in No. 10 again.

Mistress Stone — it was a traditic for St kildan men to balance o one leg on this stone and lean oc over the sea, to prove they were worthy a 'mistress'. Luckily I didn't see anyor trying this so I had to imagine it instead

St Kilda Mailboat – made out of whatever materials they had to hand, like this one drawn from a photo. Not a very reliable way of sending a letter!

The National Trust for Scotland work parties still sometimes send them out. The last one was found by two children on Shetland, and contained postcards from St Kilda.

HMS Harebell – this is the Royal Navy ship used to evacuate the St Kildans, drawn from a photo. Big ships still visit St Kilda sometimes, and we even saw a small cruise ship!

View from Conachair, the hill above the village. You can see how the village is laid out: each house has a strip of land, and the bay is very sheltered.

ST KILDA

ISLANDS AND SEA STACKS

0 ————————————————— 1
Kilometres

SOAY

Cambir

Glen Bay

Gleann Mòr

Mullach Mòr ▲ 361m

Amazon's House

Mullach Bì ▲ 358m

HMS Harebell

Mistress Stone

STAC AN ARMIN 196 m

BORERAY

172m

STAC LEE

HIRTA

376 m
nachair

Cleits

Oiseval
293 m

Main Street

School,
Church,
Manse

Pier

Village Bay

DÙN

LEVENISH

Beth Waters

Beth Waters is an author, illustrator and printmaker currently living in a tiny thatched cottage in Cambridge, UK. Originally from Yorkshire, she studied Literature at The University of Edinburgh, where she also spent a lot of time hillwalking and camping around the Highlands and islands of Scotland. Deciding to combine her love of stories with her lifelong love of drawing, she went to Cambridge School of Art to do the MA in Children's Book Illustration, and there she began to learn the art of printmaking.

Beth's work was selected for the Bologna Illustrator's Exhibition and Catalogue 2018.

Gura thall ann an Sòaigh / Across in Soay

Gura thall ann an Sòaigh
dh'fhàg mi 'n t-òganach gleusta –
urradh dhèanadh mo thacar
's tabhairt dhachaigh na sprèidhe;
tabhairt dhachaigh na sprèdhe.

It was across in Soay
that I left the nimble lad –
the one who used to provide for me
and brought home the beasts;
brought home the beasts.

Song interpreted by Anne Lorne Gillies in 2010

Many people made this book possible.

Special thanks go to the Gillies Family: John for all his support, wealth of knowledge
and enthusiasm, and Bridget and Shirley for welcoming me and sharing stories of their dad.
Thanks to all the tutors and friends at Cambridge School of Art: Martin Salisbury, Pam Smy,
Katherina Manolessou, Hannah Webb, John Williams, Josie Birch and many more. Thanks to
Susan Bain at the National Trust for Scotland, as well as the rangers and volunteers of summer
2017, for allowing us to camp on St Kilda. *Go To St Kilda* kept us safe on rough seas! Thanks to
Hilary Robinson for working her magic. Thanks to James, Sylvain, and Erik Mackie for all
their support. Thank you to my mum Cherry Waters, for everything.

All the images in this book were created by hand using printmaking techniques, before
being reproduced for publication. The technique is called monoprinting, and it is a kind
of printmaking where only one print can be produced at a time, and can't be repeated.
Ink is applied to a perspex plate using a roller or brush, and then rubbed away to create
shapes and textures. The ink is transferred to the paper using an etching press. Each colour
is printed separately and layering creates more colours. The paper needs to line up exactly
every time to create an image, and imperfections are an inherent part of the process.

Bibliography:

Gannon, A., and Geddes, G. 2015. St Kilda, The Last and Outmost Isle. Edinburgh: Historic Environment Scotland.

Gillies, A. L. 2010. Songs of Gaelic Scotland. Edinburgh: Birlinn Ltd.

Quine, D. A. 1988. St Kilda Portraits. Frome: Dowland Press Ltd.

Steel, T. 1975. The Life and Death of St Kilda. London: HarperCollins.